SPOO

SPOOKED

THE SCIENCE OF FEAR

Sylvia Funston

Illustrated by
Jane Eccles

MACMILLAN
CHILDREN'S BOOKS

First published 1996 in Canada by Owl Books

This edition first published in 1998
by Macmillan Children's Books
a division of Macmillan Publishers Ltd
25 Eccleston Place, London SW1W 9NF
and Basingstoke

Associated companies throughout the world

ISBN 0 330 35441 8

3 5 7 9 8 6 4 2

A CIP catalogue record for this book is available from
the British Library.

Printed by Mackays of Chatham plc, Chatham, Kent.

CONTENTS

INTRODUCTION

You are about to enter a world of fear and terror, a world of ghosts and goblins, of monsters, aliens and unbelievable powers. It's a world full of inexplicable things that make you shiver . . . things that aren't supposed to be. But who's to say what's supposed to be and what isn't?

When something hair-raisingly weird happens, you probably assume that it's a supernatural event – something beyond the laws of nature. Unless you're a scientist, of course. Scientists have taken on the job of trying to make sense of the world, so they can't jump to conclusions about why things happen.

What's the method scientists use to make sense of the world? First they develop scientific theories for why things happen. Then they try to produce evidence to prove their theories. But take away those theories, and sometimes scientists can be just as baffled by strange events as you.

In the spooky, scary world explored in the pages of this book you'll come across many strange creatures and events. Some have been mysteries

1

for ages, and continue to puzzle scientists because they don't fit current scientific theories. But scientists past and present (see page 101) keep searching for the truth, in the hopes of answering the question: "Are they real or are they figments of our imagination?"

Sometimes the answer is clear. Other times it's as hazy as the boundary that separates the clear, predictable world in which we live from the dark, unknown regions of the supernatural.

IT'S FRIGHT TIME!

Fear . . . that bone-melting, heart-racing, stomach-sinking feeling that reaches out and grabs you whether you expect it or not. Why does fear have to feel so gut-wrenchingly terrible? And if it feels so bad, why do we love to scare ourselves with tales of horror, monsters and bogeymen?

For some people fear can take on a whole new meaning. Seeing a dog, for instance, or looking down from the top of a tall building can trigger paralyzing terror. These exaggerated fears are called phobias. But how do they start? And what can you do about them?

Have you ever wondered why we have to feel fear at all? And why the older you get the more things you learn to fear? Take superstitions as an example. Why would sane people walk around ladders rather than under them, or knock on wood whenever a Friday falls on the 13th of the month? Did you ever wonder what frightening things these kinds of behaviours could possibly ward off?

If the thought of turning this page makes your mouth go dry, try crossing your fingers, grabbing your lucky charm or doing whatever you need to do – it's time to face down those fears . . .

3

Beware the CREEPS

Are you sitting comfortably? Looking forward to a good read? Great! Time to shake things up a bit. Take a quick look at the words at the bottom of page 7, then come right back. Now, how do you feel?

For most people, the sound of fingernails screeching on a blackboard is high on the list of things that produce an instant case of the creeps. Not far behind is the I'm-going-to-pop-any-second squeal of two balloons rubbing together. But it's not just sound that gives you the creeps. Some people hate the feel of talcum powder between their toes. Others can't bear to see caterpillars because they look so squishy. Feeling better yet?

The strange thing about the creeps is that often they are caused by things that don't seem to be dangerous. Real fear is necessary, because it helps us stay away or get away from things that will harm us. But why do we react so strongly to certain sounds, textures or sights that can't hurt us? Most experts agree that the creeps are closely connected to your "fight-or-flight" response, which works like this:

Say you're out for a walk when you come face to face with an escaped tiger from the zoo. You can pretend to be a stop sign, stay and wrestle the tiger, or run for it. While you're rooted to the spot, your brain kicks into overdrive. Deep inside your brain's fear response centre, two almond-shaped clumps of grey cells called amygdalae receive a flurry of messages from your senses

4

all saying, "That's no kitty-cat!" Your amygdalae sound the alarm and the hypothalamus in your brain responds by sending an action alert down your nerve network. Your thinking brain decides you're too short to pretend to be a stop sign and too puny to pin a tiger to the ground, so you take off at record-breaking speed.

To put your body in top escape condition, your hypothalamus sends more messages through your bloodstream, which reach your adrenal glands, perched on top of your kidneys. Luckily for you, the adrenaline these glands release gives you superhuman powers and you clear the high wall at the end of the alley in a single bound. Adrenaline is also what makes your knees shake, your teeth chatter and your heart pound!

The creeps are thought to be a mini-version of this full-fledged fight or flight response. The shuddery, jaw-clenching, heart-pounding sensation of the creeps is your reaction to a quick spurt of adrenaline triggered by your brain's response to something it recognizes as a threat. But here's the big question: what's so threatening about the sound of screeching fingernails?

Never Fear

A team of neuroscientists at the University of Iowa recently came across a woman, known as S.M., who can't recognize fear on other people's faces. When she is shown photographs of faces expressing different emotions, S.M. is baffled by those that show fear. Brain scans show that a rare disease has destroyed her amygdalae.

Scary Sounds from the Past?

One psychologist came up with an answer that reaches back beyond human history. He recorded the sound of fingernails on a blackboard and broke it down into high, middle and low frequency sounds. Then he had people react to them all. Oddly enough, it wasn't sounds at the highest frequencies that gave people the creeps, but those that fell in the middle range. What naturally occurring sounds would this range cover? The same sounds that would have scared our ancient ancestors: the danger cries of fellow primates, like the alarm call given by the vervet monkey to warn others of its kind that a predator is nearby. What other sound falls in the middle range of sound? The hair-raising sound of human screams.

Ready for Action!

Fear makes your eyes pop, your heart pound, your stomach knot and your skin turn clammy. Why?

Match the pictures showing these four body responses
to the correct reason for each, and find out.
Answers on page 99.

1 The damper your skin, the more slippery you become
and the cooler you stay when your muscles work
overtime.

2 The wider these open, the more information they can
send to your brain.

3 The faster it pumps, the more oxygen it can send to
your muscles so they can work extra hard.

4 If the muscles around it stop working, there is more
blood to send to your brain and your arm and leg
muscles.

Imagine the sound of fingernails on a blackboard

FEARS With A Capital Ph

It's normal to feel terrified when you meet an escaped tiger. But if you experience the same fear when a friendly puppy bounds up to you, you've entered the world of phobias – exaggerated, unreasonable fears.

There are four major groups of phobias. The first is agoraphobia: the fear of open spaces. Don't look for agoraphobics at a picnic in the park; they almost never leave home. Social phobias form the second group, including fear of doing things – blushing, eating, speaking or even throwing up – in public. Fear of animals comes next. The most common ones on the list slither, twitch, bark, meow, flap, scurry or dangle. The final group includes fear of objects, activities or situations – things like fuzzy tennis balls, slicing tomatoes, riding in elevators . . . well, you get the idea.

According to one theory, a phobia is born when a frightening event makes

AAGH – a puppy!

8

you remember a scary moment from early childhood. Your brain, for some reason, links the intense childhood fear with what you're experiencing years later.

A more recent theory involves a part of the left side of your brain that's known as the interpreter. Its job is to make sense of things you don't understand. Say you're watching an approaching train when suddenly you feel panic-stricken. This rush of intense emotion has nothing to do with the train. It's probably the result of an upset in your brain chemistry that just happens to coincide with the arrival of the train. But because your interpreter has the job of making sense of your scared feelings, it connects your sensation of panic to the train. Welcome to siderodromophobia, the fear of trains!

Check Your Phobias at the Door

Psychologists have discovered that if you're going to develop a phobia about animals you'll probably have it by the time you're 7. But phobias about social situations – like fear of speaking in front of a group of people – probably won't show up until you're about 15. Check with your friends and classmates and see if what they tell you agrees with this finding. And if anyone has a phobia that is making life really difficult, pass the word along that psychologists have ways to help people overcome their phobias.

Some people overcome their phobias, others decide to live with them. A Swiss farmer suffering from thalassophobia – fear of the sea – might decide the phobia isn't worth bothering about.

But what about a tightrope walker who becomes afraid of heights? Virtual reality can help. In a research study at Georgia Tech and Emory University in Atlanta, volunteer students wore virtual-reality headsets that made them feel as if they were in one of three scary situations: in a glass-walled elevator, on a balcony on a tall building and on a bridge spanning a canyon. Talk about sweaty palms and queasy stomach! But because the students were able to start at a comfortable height then slowly work their way higher, they were able to accustom themselves to heights that previously would have made them dizzy with fear. And they did it all with both feet firmly planted on the ground.

Do the Dental Drill

You love going to the dentist. Right? Wrong. But you still go — unless, of course, you're phobic about drills and other dental thrills. Psychologists at the University of Kentucky suggest that the best way to banish high dental anxiety is to find a dentist and hygienist who are trained to help you overcome your fears. They do things like play your favourite music, arrange to give you a break when you give a special hand signal, even blindfold you so that you can't see the instruments. And if you still feel faint at the thought of an injection, psychologists have special techniques that can help overcome even this.

Spot the Phobia

How's your phobia know-how? Try matching up each phobia with the picture that might trigger it. There are more pictures over the page. *Answers on page 99.*

1 Clinophobia
2 Lalophobia
3 Aerophobia
4 Ornithophobia

6 Phasmophobia
7 Musophobia
8 Arachnophobia
9 Scholionophobia
10 Ailurophobia

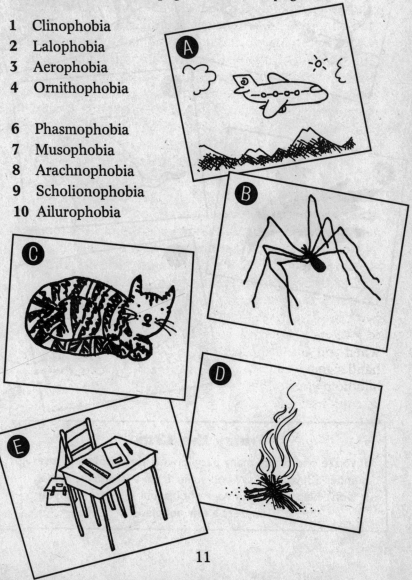

Friday the 13th

If you're one of the many people who are spooked by the number 13, you can say you suffer from triskaidekaphobia. It won't help overcome your phobia, but it might help you impress a few people.

FEARS You Can't Avoid

When you were a baby, you went through stages when you were afraid of different things. Many animals also experience built-in fears as they're growing up. Fear is a necessary part of any youngster's survival kit.

Fear of Strangers

Babies six months old and older have a built-in fear of being separated from their mothers, or chief care-givers, and are afraid of unknown faces. Both fears make sense when you remember that our early ancestors constantly moved around in search of food and shelter. Any babies who didn't cling tightly to their mothers, or who couldn't tell the difference between people who would care for them and those who wouldn't, didn't survive long. Other animals also fear strangers – chimpanzees develop fear of strangers at the same age as human babies.

Fear of Noise

Have you ever been goo-goo-gah-gahing over a baby when a sudden noise makes the baby let out an ear-splitting wail, and fling out its hands as if to grab something? Psychologists call

WWAAAH!

this the startle reflex, and we all go through a stage as infants when loud noises trigger this automatic fear response. This reflex occurs less as you get older and you begin to understand the noises of the world outside yourself. That is, until someone creeps up behind you one dark Hallowe'en and yells, "Boo!"

The Shadow Knows

An experiment done many years ago shows that humans aren't the only ones born with built-in fears. When a V-shaped shadow was moved open-end first over a two-day-old chick, it gave no reaction. But when the same V-shaped shadow was turned around so that the point led the way, the chick panicked. Why? If the shapes are moving to the right, this < matches the silhouette of a flying duck, while this > matches the silhouette of a flying hawk. The chick's reaction to the silhouette of a bird of prey must have been instinctive. Without ever having seen a hawk, the chick knew its shape spelled danger.

An experiment performed in the 1960s proved that human infants as young as six months old have an instinctive fear of falling. Researchers built a glass-topped box and taped fabric to half of the underneath surface of the glass. They taped the same fabric to the floor beneath the see-through half. A board was placed across the box, marking the division between the two halves, and babies aged 6 to 14 months were placed on the board. Every baby moved away from the see-through half and crawled onto the fabric-covered half of the glass.

Fear of Animals

The age of three seems to be a particularly fearful time for many children. It also seems to be when many children develop a fear of animals. One psychologist thinks that we can find the reason for this in our distant past. As soon as a child is old enough to explore on its own, it's much more at risk than when it is kept close to its parents. Long ago, this meant that toddlers were easy targets for predatory animals.

Other psychologists feel that young children develop a fear of animals when three built-in fears are triggered simultaneously: the fear caused by the sudden close approach of something, the fear of sudden movement and the fear of abrupt loud noise.

Cute and Cuddly

A British zoologist asked kids to name their 10 favourite animals, and they overwhelmingly chose animals with features that were human-like. All the animals they chose were mammals with large eyes and rounded faces, and all looked cuddly. Think of a giant panda, a chimpanzee or a rabbit and you've got the idea.

Are YOU Superstitious?

Have you ever jumped over a crack in the pavement or avoided walking under a ladder? If so, you're a victim of superstitious fear. But you're not alone. Millions of people, even pigeons, are superstitious. Pigeons? Absolutely! And the way pigeons develop superstitions gives us clues about ourselves.

A behavioural psychologist taught pigeons to obtain food by pecking at a button the correct number of times. The pigeons were fast learners. To keep things interesting, the psychologist decided to let the food appear at random times. No longer was there a recognizable pattern for the pigeons to learn. So what did they do? Instead of continuing to peck, they started to repeat whatever it was they were doing just before the food appeared the last time. For instance, if one of them bobbed before pecking the food-producing button, it would bob each time before it pecked.

It's just the same as you scoring a winning goal when you are wearing striped socks and thinking the striped socks helped you do it. So now you wear striped socks to every game. Of course, it was sheer coincidence that you scored a goal *and* wore striped socks on the same day. But your brain, in trying to make sense of what happened, was willing to accept a supernatural explanation if it couldn't find a natural one. Maybe the same interpreter in your left brain that plays a part in creating phobias also helps superstitious beliefs to grow.

Who's Superstitious Here?

The scene overleaf is full of superstitious people. What's the superstition each one believes? Match each one to the correct explanation. *Answers on page 99.*

1   The ancient Greeks thought this substance held life because it could preserve food. To avert bad luck when it spilled, you were supposed to throw some over your left shoulder, hitting evil spirits there in the eye.

2   Do this when you brag about something, so you won't offend the fates. In ancient times, if you wanted the protection of powerful tree gods, you knocked on a tree – but it had to be with your right hand.

3 This animal is probably the world's most famous bad luck symbol – except in Britain, where it's supposed to be lucky. Why is it bad luck elsewhere? It's probably its colour – the colour of night and the powers of darkness.

4 Long ago, people thought they saw their souls in their reflections. Breaking one of these was supposed to bring bad luck lasting seven years – since the human mind and body was thought to renew itself every seven years.

5 Bad luck beliefs about this might go back to a Norse legend in which a god gate-crashed a feast given for 12 gods. Trouble broke out, causing the death of everyone's favourite god. In China, it is considered very lucky.

6 When this leans against a wall it forms a triangle, the sacred symbol of life. Walking through a triangle was thought to put your life in danger. To undo the bad luck, keep your fingers crossed until you see a dog!

7 This superstition probably started during Roman times, when many illnesses were fatal. Sneezing could be the first sign that someone had caught anything from the flu to the bubonic plague.

8 Doing this to remember something follows an ancient belief that a knot was a charm against evil. If a demon saw the knot, it would become intrigued by the knot's complex shape and forget about bothering you.

9 Superstitions about this direction are linked to the ancient ritual of sun worship. Sun-worshippers believed that important functions should be done in an east-to-west direction, following the path of the sun.

10 Hundreds of years ago people thought these represented the openings of graves, maybe even family graves.

Friday Drivers

Friday the 13th really does seem to be hazardous to your health. A recent study by British researchers shows that road accidents sent more drivers to the hospital on Fridays that fell on the 13th than on any other Friday. Motorists stood a 52 percent greater chance of being hospitalized on Friday the 13th than they did on the previous Friday. Perhaps everyone should take public transport on the unlucky 13th – or better yet, stay in bed until the 14th.

Did You Know?

If anyone books a table for 13 people at London's famous Savoy Hotel, staff bring the ceramic "Savoy Black Cat" to the table to be the 14th guest.

TERRORS OF THE NIGHT

There's something about the dark that brings out our worst fear — the one that something dangerous is lurking in the shadows, ready to pounce on us the moment we let down our guard.

Is this fear from far in the past, when the dark was filled with the sounds of sharp-toothed, long-clawed animals prowling the forests from dusk to dawn? Is it the basis of our belief in bogeymen, werewolves, vampires and other nightstalkers? The night is a reminder of our ancient terror that some of us can control the powers of darkness or change into predatory animals. Or even worse . . . that you might wake up one red sunset as a vampire that must feed on blood.

On the other hand, if the dark frightens us so much, why do we associate the light-giving full moon with werewolves and other bogeymen of the night? And does it really have the power to drive people mad?

Ready for the terrors of the night? Maybe you should grab some garlic first, and sharpen your stake . . .

Once Upon a Scary Time

Long ago, fairy tales weren't told to entertain children; they were used to teach valuable lessons about life. And the hair-raising mix of fantasy and horror made sure they had an eager audience. Scary stories can actually help you overcome your fears. How? Take the story of Jack and the Beanstalk. Jack outsmarts the giant who wants to grind up his bones to make bread. The giant's threat thrills you and fills you with relief that it's not happening to you. When Jack triumphs, you're sure that if you keep your wits about you, you too can overpower the mean giants in your life and conquer your worst fears.

It's BOO Time

Think back a few years. Did you used to check under your bed before you got into it? Sleep with a night light? Close the wardrobe door so that you couldn't see the bogeyman looming there? Don't be embarrassed – just about everyone is afraid of the dark at one time or another. But why?

Maybe we should look to our early ancestors for a possible answer. They didn't live in houses or apartments with sturdy doors they could lock at night. Their only protection against the unseen dangers of the night was to climb high into a tree and hope that nothing hungry could reach them. Is it possible, as one famous psychiatrist suggests, that all humans still share a memory of these terrifying times – but a memory so dim we don't even recognize it as a memory?

Boo!

Bwgwl (pronounced *bugul*) is an ancient Welsh word that means "object of terror." In northern England and Scotland the same word became *bugaboos*, in France *bugibus*, and in Germany *boggleman*. Yes, you've guessed it – the *bwgwl* is the *bogeyman*!

Monkey Fears

Humans belong to the primate family, and many primates still live in trees. Infant baboons seem to share our fear of the dark. And with good reason. Sunset is the cue for hungry hunters to begin their stealthy, night-long prowls. Baboons are also afraid of snakes and of falling – after all, snakes are natural enemies of mammals, and a fall from a treetop or cliff could be fatal.

Our dreams might contain other clues that explain our fear of the dark. College students were asked by psychologists to list their most common dreams. Dreaming about falling came top of the list, followed by dreams of being chased. And almost half of everyone surveyed reported dreaming about snakes. Is it possible that dreams somehow reveal ancient memories that are stored beyond the reach of our waking minds?

The Bogeyman Will Get You!

Most people aren't so much afraid of the dark as they are of the unseen things that might be lurking in it – whether these monsters surface in dreams or are creations of the imagination. Remember the terrifying figure in the wardrobe that turned out to be a pile of clothes and other junk once the light was turned on? Once upon a time it was usual for parents to tell their children that the bogeyman would get them if they didn't behave. Just think of the millions of kids who must have shivered themselves to sleep on countless nights, not daring to make a sound in case that big, shambling creature of shadows got them.

Today, most parents would never think of threatening

their children with the bogeyman. Yet kids around the world are still afraid of unseen terrors in the dark. The bogeyman takes many shapes – from goblins and trolls to werewolves and vampires, even aliens from outer space. Could all these creatures be our way of dealing with the ancient human memory of being hunted in the night?

Bogeys Under the Bed

A psychologist at the University of California asked children where to look for bogeymen. More girls than boys replied, "Under the bed!" He thinks that millions of years ago our female ancestors spent more time in trees than males did, so now girls have more fear of things coming from beneath them. Other scientists feel we would have lost these behaviours a long time ago. But the psychologist claims other things support his theory. Watching kids in a playground, he found that girls spent more time than boys playing on climbing equipment. And another thing — why do girls often pull their feet up under them during the really freaky parts of scary movies?

It's a HOWL!

At one time or another, people all over the world have believed that humans could change into animals. In Japan, shape-shifters change back and forth between human form and the shapes of rabbits, cats, foxes and badgers. Foxes are popular among Chinese shape-shifters too. In India and Cambodia, it was thought people could take on the shape of tigers to become weretigers. Northern countries have werebears; and different parts of Africa have werelions, werecrocodiles and even weresharks. Europe seems to specialize in werewolves.

Why wolves? Long ago, winter nights were long and intensely dark. People knew that just beyond the walls of their simple homes were the wild woods and the wolves. When food was scarce in the forest, wolves would be driven by hunger into the villages, hunting for anything they could eat. Usually they attacked only the livestock. But there's a report that during the bitterly cold winter of 1450, starving wolves crept through a hole in the walls around the city of Paris and killed 40 people.

Today, the terrifying dark and the wild, tangled woods are gone. So are the wolves, hunted almost to extinction in many parts of the world. But stories like Little Red Riding Hood and The Three Little Pigs introduce us to the Big Bad Wolf when we are very young. These stories keep alive deep, dark memories of wolves as strong, intelligent animals that threaten us.

A Hair-raising Story

In medieval times, some witches would cover themselves with an ointment made from a plant called wolfsbane, thinking that it had the power to change them into wolves. Scientists now know that wolfsbane contains ingredients that can irritate the nerve endings in the skin. The result? Users of the ointment felt as if the hair on their skin was rising.

If wolves are frightening, then werewolves are positively terrifying. People have been writing about werewolves since the time of the ancient Greeks. There were many ways a person could become a howling success as a wolf. For instance, witches were supposed to be able to change into wolves, and to be able to change anyone else into one, too. In some parts of the world you could become wolfish just by sleeping on the ground in an open field on a Friday night when the moon was full. (So much for that weekend camping trip you were planning?) In other parts of the world, eating meat from a sheep that had been killed by a wolf, drinking water from a wolf's footprint, or throwing on a wolf skin would have you howling at the moon in no time.

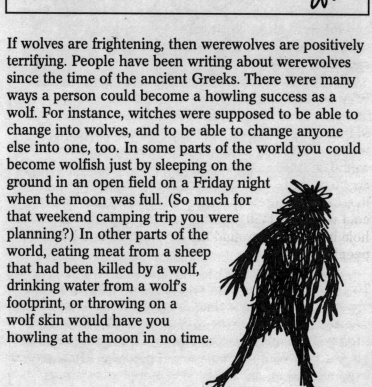

Wolfman?

Jo-Jo, above, was one of the most famous people to suffer from a rare disease called hypertrichosis. Symptoms range from hairy patches on the skin to hair everywhere except for the palms of the hands, the soles of the feet and the lips. Some men with hypertrichosis shave their faces several times a day. Others, like Jo-Jo, used to earn a living as "wolfmen" in the circus. An American geneticist thinks this extreme hairiness is a throwback to the time when we all were covered in hair. Face and body hair in humans disappeared as we no longer needed it for warmth and protection. But just because we lost most of our hair doesn't mean we lost the "hairy gene" that makes it grow. In rare cases, this gene gets turned on — with spectacular results.

It's in Your Blood

Fangs, fur and a ferocious temper: the horror movies have taught us all what to expect, even if science says werewolves can't exist. A biochemist at the University of British Columbia thinks that werewolf stories might be based on more than superstition and scary movies. His explanation has to do with a chemical known as porphyrin – the stuff that makes your blood red. When the porphyrin in your blood doesn't work properly, you suffer from a disease called porphyria. King George III was one of its most famous victims.

There are eight types of porphyria and one of them produces symptoms that sound strangely familiar. People with this kind of porphyria only use a small amount of the porphyrin their bodies produce. The rest is stored in their bones or under their skin. It becomes a problem when the victim goes out into the sunlight. Then the porphyrin changes the oxygen in the skin into a harmful form – to the point where noses and fingers can fall off. This kind of porphyria also makes body hair grow profusely, and the victim's gums and lips grow tight and draw back from the teeth, so that the teeth appear larger than normal. It causes flat noses, fangs and hairy, pawlike hands! Is it any wonder that people thought the poor person with these symptoms was a werewolf?

Full MOON Rising

According to legend, it's only when the moon is full that a normal, law-abiding citizen turns into a killer werewolf. Of course, this probably has to do with the fact that wolves hunt most successfully in bright moonlight.

Yet there are mysteries about the moon that have been sensed by people for thousands of years. What kind of power does the moon have over life on earth? And is this power real, or is it all in our imagination?

What if the Moon Didn't Exist?

Astronomers suggest that life on earth would be very different.

● Tides would be one-third as high
● The planet would rotate faster, so days might be only eight hours long
● Strong nonstop winds would create higher ocean waves
● Hurricanes would occur more frequently and would be more powerful
● Plants and animals would have to change their shapes and lifestyles to handle very windy eight-hour days
● Without moonlight, animals that hunt, forage or mate by the light of the moon would never evolve.

Hmm . . . makes you look at the moon in a new light, doesn't it?

The Big Pull

Think of the moon as an 80,000,000,000,000,000,000-tonne magnet, one that circles the earth three-days' journey away. As this moon magnet sweeps across the planet's surface it pulls both water and land toward it. In the oceans this pull creates tides. But did you also know that the entire continent of North America can rise by as much as 15 cm (6 inches) when the moon is directly above it?

If the moon can have this big an impact on our planet, can it also affect us? After all, we are 80 percent water and 20 percent solid, which is the same proportion as water to land on the surface of the earth. Scientific studies seem to confirm what psychiatrists, ambulance drivers, and police have long suspected: more people are admitted to mental hospitals and more crime is committed when the moon is full than at any other time during the lunar month. No wonder the word *lunacy*, or craziness – that also gives us *loony* – comes from *luna*, the Latin word for moon. So it seems the moon does have the power to affect our behaviour, but exactly how that works is still a mystery.

Moon Beams and Oysters

If the moon affects people, what about animals? Oysters open their shells at high tide. Do they tell from the ebb and flow of the tide when to open, or do they use some other cue? To find out, a biologist shipped oysters by air from the coast of Connecticut to his laboratory in Evanston, Illinois. For the first week the oysters opened their shells when the tide was high in Connecticut. Towards the end of the second week, however, they began to open their shells when the moon was directly over Evanston. If Evanston were a coastal city, it would experience high tide at that time. Somehow the oysters seemed to sense the gravitational pull of the moon and opened their shells when it was at its strongest.

Loony but True

Dental researchers at the University of North Carolina have recently added fresh bite to the old legend that a full moon causes teeth to grow. It seems that kids' teeth do grow mostly at night, during sleep. Had any night time urges to howl at the moon?

CREATURES of the Night

I t's safe to say that the California vampire researcher who offered $10,000 to anyone who could produce an authentic live human vampire can keep his money. Vampires are dead. Of course, that's the whole point. Legend says a vampire is a dead person who refuses to stay dead, who feeds on the blood of the living and lurks in dark shadows avoiding the light of day. How could this superstitious belief develop all around the world? The answer might lie in two very different diseases.

Tuberculosis is now pretty rare through most of the world, but this disease caused a lot of people to weaken and die before doctors found ways to prevent and treat it. Two U.S. pathologists claim that some grisly remains in a Connecticut cemetery suggest a connection between tuberculosis and vampire superstitions, and show that New Englanders probably believed in vampires as recently as the last century.

Folklore said that anyone dying of tuberculosis would return as a vampire to feed on the blood of family members, who would then waste away and die. The only way to save the family was to burn the vampire's heart or its whole body. If the heart was missing, the bones were rearranged to prevent the vampire from rising again. When the pathologists opened the 19th-century grave of a middle-aged man, they discovered that his skull and thighbones had been rearranged on top of his ribs – which showed evidence of a tuberculosis infection. Not understanding that tuberculosis spreads quickly in crowded living conditions, the farmers turned to a supernatural explanation for the way victims of tuberculosis wasted away, as if their blood were being drained.

Porphyria, which helped brand its sufferers as werewolves, is the second disease that could partly account for the belief in vampires. If people with a certain form of porphyria go out into the sun, excess porphyrin in their skin absorbs light and then re-emits it later. The result? They glow in the dark. Believe it or not, the treatment for this illness is an injection of haem – the iron-rich part of your red blood cells. Yes, a dose of blood!

News from Vampire Central

The director of the Vampire Research Center in Elmhurst, New York, says that, contrary to popular belief, vampires can go out in daylight — with the right protection. "They just need to wear a sun block of SPF 15 or higher," he stated.

A Grave Mistake

Remember the character of The Count from *Sesame Street*? Even though he was helpful and harmless, his black cape, fangs, Eastern European accent and fondness for bats marked him as a vampire. This image of vampires comes from the book *Dracula*, written in 1897 by Bram Stoker. And Bela Lugosi's portrayal of Count Dracula in the movies taught us most of what we know about vampires.

*

At night vampires rise from their graves, but they return to sleep in their coffins as soon as the sun rises. Where did this idea come from? Imagine this: you're living in 16th-century Europe. Someone in your village gets ill, and one morning she's found without any signs of life. Once she's buried as dead, people start suspecting she's a vampire. The villagers gather to dig up the body so it can be burned. Imagine the horror when you open the coffin to find her clothes in disarray and her fingers all bloody. As a superstitious peasant living 400 years ago, you would think a corpse that showed signs of leaving the grave to walk around, and of drinking blood, must be a vampire, right? Think again.

Until fairly recently, doctors had no sure way of telling whether a patient was really dead or deep in a coma, or even suffering from catalepsy, an illness that makes the victim appear dead. Occasionally, people were buried alive. How awful it would be for them to wake up in coffins deep underground, and to spend their last hours trying to scratch their way out. People finally understood about premature burial and doctors learned to detect life signs in comatose or cataleptic patients, and the numbers of "vampires" dropped — except in superstition.

Wonder Bulb

It's thought that vampires can't stand garlic. And no wonder. This wonder bulb acts as a powerful antibiotic, prevents blood from clotting, lowers blood pressure, is good for your heart, and might even help fight off cancer. And garlic also seems to boost your brain's production of serotonin, which makes you feel happy. It's enough to make a self-respecting vampire hang up its cloak and call it a night.

Believe it or not . . .

Scientists are using the saliva from vampire bats to produce a drug that prevents blood from clotting. They hope that it will help save the lives of stroke victims. It's nice to know scientists have a sense of humour. They've named this new drug Draculin.

BEWITCHED

We're all familiar with the scary witch of Hallowe'en, the witch we love to hate. Ugly, old and warty, this bogeywoman wears a pointy black hat and flies a state-of-the-art broomstick. Her constant companion is her familiar – usually a black cat – that helps her work magic. She casts evil spells that make people ill or force them to do crazy things.

The power of our belief in witches is so strong that even portrayals of them are supposed to bring bad luck. Shakespeare's play *Macbeth* has a famous scene showing three witches gathering around their cauldron to concoct evil. Superstition holds that the song they sing in this scene must not be sung anywhere but onstage. It is said to have the power to work evil

because Shakespeare used real witches' curses to impress King James I, who had a fascination with the strange and spooky.

Where did our image of the evil witch come from? Actually, it's a warped version of the "crone," a wise old goddess of an ancient religion called Wicca, pronounced "witcha." In 1484, Pope Innocent VIII tried to stamp out Wicca by officially declaring all Wiccans agents of the Devil. For the next 200 years, people suspected of being witches – most of them women – were tortured to make them confess and were often burned at the stake. As many as 200,000 women might have been burned alive in Europe during the infamous witch hunts of the Middle Ages. Many of these "witches" were killed simply because they were midwives who helped women deliver their babies, or herbalists who knew how to treat illness with plants.

Magic Root

In the Middle Ages, midwives helped women through childbirth, using natural medicines like the root of the mandrake plant. The mandrake root is shaped something like a human body, and was said to scream when dug out of the ground. The mandrake root calms down people who eat it as a medicine. This ability to change people's behaviour, combined with its strange "human" qualities, led superstitious people to believe that it was a magic root. Today, of course, doctors know mandrake as a source of scopolamine, a powerful drug renowned for its soothing effect on people who are anxious or upset — especially those who suffer from motion sickness.

The Real Salem Witch?

An outbreak of "witchcraft" in Salem, Massachusetts, and other nearby villages, began in 1692. Two girls, aged 9 and 11, started to act in ways that shocked the communities. One girl fell on the floor in convulsions, arms and legs jerking out of control, or threw the Bible across the room. The other disrupted prayers with her shrieks, and threw pieces of burning wood from the fire around the room. A group of older girls started making wild gestures and talking nonsense. They said they felt as if they were being pinched and bitten. People decided that these innocent girls must be the victims of witchcraft. In all, 150 people were accused of bewitching the girls and, of these, 95 were executed.

When a psychology student at the University of California at Santa Barbara read about the Salem witchcraft affair, she wondered if a natural cause could have triggered the events that led to the trials. After finding out what people in Salem would have eaten, her research led her to a fungus, called ergot, that sometimes poisons rye grown on moist, shaded land. If you eat ergot, the symptoms range from mild ones such as nausea, the feeling that ants are crawling under the skin, and muscle twitches, to serious ones such as painful spasms, convulsions, the inability to pass urine, hallucinations, and even death. Many of these symptoms match those described by people who claimed to be under the spell of witches.

Outbreaks of ergot poisoning in Europe throughout the Middle Ages were often accompanied by witchcraft persecutions. Was ergot-poisoned rye bread the real witch of Salem? Maybe . . . so could an outbreak of ergot poisoning happen today? Because farmers now know about ergot, the rye bread you buy today is perfectly safe. Go ahead and make yourself a peanut butter and spell sandwich on rye.

Full Moon Madness

Ever noticed how the moon is larger when it's close to the horizon than when it's high in the sky? It helps to be a bit loony when you try to find out why. Just be sure to wait until the moon is full . . .

Loony Test 1

Ask permission to use an aspirin-sized pill for this experiment. Go outside when the moon is close to the horizon. Hold the pill out at arm's length between you and the moon. How much of the moon's face does it cover? Wait  until the moon is high in the sky and repeat the experiment. Now how much of the moon's face does the pill cover?

Loony Test 2

Take a sheet of paper outside when the full moon is on the horizon. Roll the paper into a tube with the same diameter as the face of the moon. That is, the moon should fit snugly into the end of the tube when you look through it. Tape both ends of the tube so that its diameter doesn't change. Wait until the moon is high, and repeat the experiment. Does the moon's face still fill the end of the tube?

Loony Test 3

Look at the full moon on the horizon. Big isn't it? Now turn your back on it, bend down and look at it upside-down through your legs. (Who's loony now?) Has it changed size?

Answers on page 100.

Did You Know?

We set our clocks by the sun, but our bodies often want to follow the timing of the moon. A human pregnancy lasts 266 days. This is 9 months made up of 29.5 days each — the exact number of days it takes for the moon to travel through its four phases.

THINGS THAT GO BUMP

Mention the supernatural, and the first thoughts to float through your head are probably of ghosts and goblins! Most people these days don't believe in goblins or fairies, but ghosts are another matter. Are ghosts really the spirits of dead people? Ghostbusting scientists are doing some spooky research to discover just what these apparitions are all about.

And then there are poltergeists – literally, "noisy ghosts." They're the smash and crash experts of the phantom world. Some researchers claim that poltergeist pranks result when someone's telepathic powers go wrong. And that someone is usually a teenager with attitude. Forget the ghosts, now we're into mind power.

Extrasensory perception, or ESP, takes us into a world where words, telephones, computers, pens, paper and all the other normal means of communicating ideas are completely unnecessary. But can people really beam thoughts to each other or make objects move simply by willing them to? And what about animals? If people have ESP, could pets be psychic, too? You don't have to read minds to find out the answers to all these questions – just keep reading this book . . .

PHANTOMS and Fairies

Long ago, just about everyone believed in ghosts, the spirits of the dead appearing to the living. But then, 100 years ago many people believed that fairies were real, too. People combined their interest in supernatural apparitions with the new hobby of photography, and pictures like the photo below were very popular.

Ghost of child at grieving mother's feet.

Fairies Photographed!

Would you have believed this headline in a 1920 issue of London's *Strand Magazine*? What if you knew that the author was Sir Arthur Conan Doyle, creator of the famous fictional detective Sherlock Homes? Doyle believed in fairies, and published the photos taken by 16-year-old Elsie Wright showing herself and 10-year-old Frances Griffiths with tiny, winged sprites (above). Were the fairies real, or the photos faked? The mystery remained unsolved until 60 years later, when computer enhancement of the pictures showed that none of the fairies had any depth. Unless fairies are completely flat, the girls faked the photos. In 1982, Elsie Wright confessed they had drawn fairies on paper, cut them out and stuck them to tree branches with pins. But right up to the day she died, Frances Griffiths insisted that a photograph showing two almost translucent fairies was real.

Some people still believe in ghosts. But scientists have their own ideas about the source of ghostly noises or sightings. Some of them are as amazing as the ghosts they're trying to explain, while others – well, take the case of the haunted house in Yorkshire . . .

The banging noises had been going on for months. Not even the police could solve the mystery of the strange noises. There seemed only one thing left to think: the place must be haunted!

But when a team of researchers investigated the house they found some very unghostlike clues. Deep cracks in the walls, twisted door frames and a sagging roof suggested that the house was shifting on its foundations. Outside, they found an unused sewer that passed close to the house and connected with the river. They'd found the "ghost." At each high tide, water was forced up the sewer and seeped into the sandy soil under the house. This daily soaking made the soil unstable and caused the house to shift and settle, creating some very unearthly noises in the process!

A Slip in Time

One day in the 1960s, a plumber named Harry Martindale was working in the cellar of the Treasurer's House in York. It was lunchtime and he was alone. Suddenly, a bugle sounded and through the walls of the cellar marched more than 20 Roman soldiers and a cart-horse. Martindale described them as walking *in* the floor because he could not see below their knees. Excavations beneath the building later revealed that the Via Decumana, the ancient road that led to York's first Roman fortress, ran across the cellar about 45 cm (18 inches) below its floor. The road must have been used constantly by soldiers a thousand years earlier. Did Harry Martindale see a replay of a historic event? Or was he somehow existing both in the 1960s and in ancient England at the same time? Can objects exist in two times at the same place any more than they can exist in two places at the same time? One of the laws of physics is that an object can be in only one place at a time, and scientists believe that everything you can see, from the tip of your nose to the farthest star, obeys the laws of physics. But as soon as you start probing into things too small to see – inside the atom – the laws of physics get turned upside-down. Books and bicycles might have to stay rooted to the spot, but subatomic (smaller than an atom) particles can be in several places at once! What this all has to do with the ghosts of Roman soldiers is anyone's guess, but it does suggest that things might not always be what they appear to be.

A Waking Dream?

If you ever come across a ghost and there's something strange about the sky or the light, pinch yourself. You might be experiencing a waking dream: you think you're receiving information through your senses from your surroundings, but instead you're receiving it from your dreaming brain. It's a bit like watching closed-circuit TV.

WELCOME to ESP

There are many reports of someone seeing the ghost of a friend or relative only to discover later that the person they saw died at the exact same time. Some scientists think that this is just a hallucination, a vision created in the brain of the person who "sees" the apparition, remembered later as coinciding with the loved one's death. Other people suggest that telepathy, or mind to mind communication, might be involved. The idea is that one person projects a telepathic image, which is received by someone else, who then "sees" the sender or "gets a message" from the sender. How it all happens is a mystery, but it definitely beats e-mail.

In case you hadn't sensed it, you're entering the world of extrasensory perception (ESP) – where people supposedly can obtain information through some kind of sense beyond the ones we use to see, hear, touch, smell, taste and know where our bodies are in space.

Are You "Encounter-Prone?"

Two psychologists at Cushing Hospital in Framingham, Massachusetts, have found that about 1 person in 20 has an extremely active imagination. Their findings seem to be backed up by two researchers from the University of Connecticut who claim that some people are "encounter-prone," much more likely than others to imagine meeting ghosts or aliens.

ESP covers several strange talents in addition to telepathy: psychokinesis (the ability to use mind power to affect objects); precognition (seeing into the future); clairvoyance (the ability to see things happening over a great distance); clairaudience and clairsentience (the ability to hear and feel things happening far away). Parapsychologists have been testing ESP in laboratories since 1930, but except for one or two notable findings, they have so far failed to prove that ESP exists.

Mystery Train

During the 1950s an American researcher looked at records of railway accidents in which 10 or more people were injured. He noted how many passengers were travelling on the trains when they crashed, then looked back at the records for the same trains from one week before the accident. He discovered that significantly fewer people, on average, were travelling on the trains on the days of the accidents than on the same train routes the week before. What did he conclude? Perhaps passengers had a premonition that something bad would happen, and decided not to travel on that particular train on that day.

Noisy Ghosts

In March 1984, strange things started happening in a house in Columbus, Ohio. Lights and taps switched on and off on their own, glasses smashed on the floor, eggs flew up and broke on the ceiling, and candles, lamps and knick-knacks began to move. Not so long ago, people would have assumed that a poltergeist – a "noisy ghost" – was at work. But a team of researchers from the Psychical Research Foundation in North Carolina thought there might be another cause, and agreed to investigate.

The team spent six days in the house with the family. Finally, they decided that the clue to the mystery was the family's teenage daughter, who had been going through a difficult time with her parents. The researchers believed that the daughter's strong, painful emotions were somehow affecting objects around her. Testing in the laboratory revealed that her brain was producing abnormal brain waves. Could it be that instructions from the girl's brain, which would normally go to her body, were somehow reaching objects around her?

No one knows whether disturbed teenagers really can whiz things around using mind power alone – a process known as psychokinesis or PKI for short. And nobody knows whether telepathy really does let people see apparitions at the time of someone's death. But scientists are getting results from some carefully controlled experiments on psychokinesis and telepathy that are making non-believers take note . . .

How Did He Do That?

On July 19, 1759 — long before instant satellite feeds, TV news, fax machines, even telephones — Emmanuel Swedenborg amazed the people of Göteborg in Sweden by updating them through the day on the progress of a disastrous fire. What's so amazing about that, you might ask? Only that this particular fire was sweeping through Stockholm, 480 km (298 miles) away. Two days later, a messenger arrived from Stockholm and confirmed everything Swedenborg had said!

It's a TOSS-UP

Look Ma, No Hands!

At Wright-Patterson Air Force Base near Dayton, Ohio, a man climbs into a flight simulator. His task is to make the simulator tip, or bank, by making a green line cover up a black line on the screen in front of him. But there's a catch. He's connected to the simulator by wires attached to electrodes on his scalp, and he's not allowed to use anything but brain power to control it. He does it using his eyes. On each side of the screen is a flickering light. The visual cortex at the back of his brain processes everything he sees, and responds to the flickers with bursts of electricity. By speeding up the electrical bursts, he banks the simulator to the right. And by slowing them down, he banks to the left. It's not ESP, since his brain is wired to the machine, and ESP is supposed to work without actual physical connections. But just imagine where this research could lead — mind-powered wheelchairs, video games, musical instruments . . .

For the past 15 years, when he hasn't been figuring out how to get people to Mars, a rocket scientist at Princeton University has been conducting an experiment using a "random-event generator." Think of it as a very fast machine that can do the electronic equivalent of tossing a coin 1,000 times each second. The rules of chance say that these "coins" should fall heads-up half the time and tails-up the other half. In the experiment, people try to use their mind power — or PKI — to make the random-event generator produce more than 50 percent heads or tails. After 14 million trials using 100 different people, the results showed that for every 1,000 electronic "coin tosses," the generator produced one more head or tail than chance says it should. This might not sound like much to you, but it caused a lot of talk among scientists. It suggests that your mind might be able to influence things outside of itself — even if it's only in very small ways.

Are You Receiving Me?

For seven years, a researcher at the Psychophysical Research Laboratories in New Jersey conducted telepathy experiments with people trying to send and receive telepathic messages. The scientist tried to eliminate any chance of cheating, accidental or otherwise, by enclosing the "sender" and "receiver" in soundproof cubicles. Then he covered the eyes of the receiver and made him wear headphones playing the soft hissing sound of white noise. That way, the receiver's brain could not pick up information through sight or sound.

After about 15 minutes of not seeing or hearing anything, most people's brains begin to create their own images. The researcher believed that if telepathy really did exist, images from the sender might turn up among the receiver's hallucinations. While the sender concentrated on images that appeared on a screen in his cubicle, the receiver described out loud what he was seeing inside his head. During some trials the sender would see a photograph on the screen, other times he saw video clips. The images were picked randomly by a computer. At the end of each session, the receiver looked at a collection of photographs or video clips. Some had been used in the experiment, others had not. He was asked to pick the ones that best matched things he'd seen in his head. If all he did was guess, he'd be right 25 percent of the time.

When he looked at the photographs he was right only 27 percent of the time – barely better than chance. But when he looked at the video clips, he was right about 40 percent of the time! Like the PKI experiments at Princeton University, these experiments on telepathy seem to suggest that something other than chance is happening. But what it is, and how to prove it, still eludes scientists.

What's the Frequency?

The reason one astronomer thinks that human brains might have the potential for telepathy is that they give off weak but measurable radio waves!

PET ESP?

You've probably heard stories of pets that seem to know exactly what their owners are thinking. And the news often contains stories about strange animal behaviour that was later seen to be advance warning of an earthquake. Do animals have ESP, or are there more ordinary explanations for their sometimes extraordinary behaviour? Research studies seem to show that dogs can be very aware of their owners.

Jaytee is a five-year-old terrier who belongs to a woman in Lancashire. Jaytee always seems to know when his owner is coming home, and a team of researchers captured evidence on film. One film crew accompanied Jaytee's owner when she left home and another crew recorded what Jaytee was doing while she was gone.

Neither the crew back home nor the dog's owner knew when she would return, since the time was decided randomly by the crew that went with her. And to avoid the possibility of Jaytee recognizing the sound of her car on the return journey, his owner took a taxi home. So what happened?

Jaytee moved around a lot during the three hours his owner was away. But at the moment she was told to return home by taxi, the little terrier got up, walked to the window and sat down. He was still sitting there when she arrived. As with all scientific experiments, however, one success isn't enough to prove anything. So more experiments are being planned with other pets to see if their "sixth sense" behaviour can also be captured on film.

Doctor Dog's Diagnosis

People who suffer from epilepsy can lose consciousness and hurt themselves when they fall. American and British researchers are looking into the possibility that dogs might be able to detect subtle physical changes in their owners that warn of an impending epileptic seizure. One dog owner in Maine sits down somewhere safe when his dog barks urgently at him because he's learned that it's a 10-minute advance warning of an attack. Meanwhile, in Liverpool, another dog gives his owner a 30-minute warning by giving one short bark and walking nervously around. Are both these dogs picking up altered brain waves from their owners? Or are they noticing subtle behaviours or changes in body chemistry that alter the way their owners smell? Only more research will tell.

Shake, Rattle and Moo

For several years, a professor of physical chemistry at Berlin's Free University gathered information about animals doing unusual things just before an earthquake strikes. He concluded that many animals are able to sense an approaching earthquake. But they don't seem to need a sixth sense to do it.

Animals' normal senses are so acute they can do the job on their own. For example, it's thought that some animals are able to hear the very small tremors that occur before a quake and which humans cannot detect. Certain animals are very sensitive to the vibrations these tremors produce. Others might also be able to detect electrical changes that occur when rocks deep underground are put under enormous pressure.

Some Drumsticks!

A pigeon's legs contain more than a hundred tiny vibration sensors, smaller than grains of rice and connected by a network of nerves. Researchers discovered that these vibration sensors give the pigeon advance warning of earth tremors.

Animals Do the Strangest Things

Which of these things do you think animals might do before an earthquake strikes? *Answer on page 100.*

1 Ants move their eggs out of anthills.

2 Pigs bite each other.

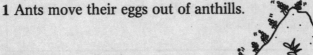

ouch!

3 Frogs stop croaking.

4 Snakes wriggle
out of their dens.

5 Goldfish in aquariums
swim around frantically.

6 Dogs howl.

7 Catfish jump around
in the water.

8 Rats roam the streets.

9 Cats leave home.

10 Cows fight each other.

All in the MIND?

When something happens that people can't explain, they often assume it is paranormal, or outside the realm of normal reality. But events that are out of the ordinary can have normal explanations. Take OBEs, or out-of-body experiences, in which people feel themselves existing and even travelling outside their bodies. When one psychologist in England felt herself float across the world, leaving her body behind, it was an experience so vivid she decided to do research into out-of-body experiences.

She found that out-of-body experiences can have natural causes; for example, stress on the brain can create a floating sensation. She began to think that "paranormal illusions" result from the way our brains misinterpret what we experience. Your brain tries to find meaning in unusual events the same way it tries to make sense of an optical illusion. You see the sloping lines of the wall in the picture at left, and your brain inteprets them to mean the wall recedes into the distance. Your brain makes sense of the scene by seeing each of the three soldiers as taller than the one to the left of him. Even when you understand this optical illusion, it's very hard to override your brain's interpretation, and to see that each soldier is exactly the same height.

If your brain can't find meaning in what it sees, it creates it. Perhaps, the psychologist concluded, it does the same thing to create meaning for what it experiences. If your brain feels as if you're floating, it assumes that you actually are floating. It interprets the event as something taking place in some sort of paranormal reality, instead of just in your head.

People tend to think that an event is paranormal if it seems too unlikely to have happened by coincidence. Like the time you were thinking of a long-lost friend just before she called you. Was it a coincidence or was ESP involved? When confronted with something they don't understand, people consider the probability of it having natural or unnatural causes. The most accurate way to determine probabilities is to use mathematics. But most people don't and, because of this, their judgement of whether something happens by coincidence or not is usually terrible!

Losing Your Marbles

How good are you at guessing probabilities? A paper bag contains 10 red marbles and 10 blue marbles. Imagine that, with your eyes closed, you pull out 10 marbles, 8 of which are red. What colour marble are you most likely to pull out next?

Answer on page 100.

Psychic Dreams

Here's another example. Say you dream that one of your favourite sports heroes is killed in a terrible accident. The next day, the news is full of the tragedy. You decide it's all too much of a coincidence to be merely chance and that you have ESP.

But just a minute! A British statistician worked out how often this kind of dream should come true, strictly by chance. He based his calculations on Britain's population and assumed that each one of its 55 million people had only one death dream in a lifetime. His conclusion was that every two weeks, purely by chance, someone would dream of someone else's death and it would coincide with that death.

So the next time you're approaching a red light in the family car, forget about thinking that you can control the lights. If the lights change to green before you get there, it's still purely chance that it happened while you were beaming intense thought rays saying, "Change now, change now, change now . . . "

The Purple Smell of Grass

Eyes see, ears hear, tongues taste and skin feels — and that's all there is to it. Right? Wrong. Some people have "crossed wires" when it comes to senses. They might see colours when they read words. Others might taste words and still others might feel textures and shapes when they taste things. This condition, called synesthesia, is unusual but not as paranormal as it might seem. One prominent neurologist thinks synesthesia is a normal brain process that most of us just don't use, but many other scientists disagree.

Do YOU Have ESP?

You'll need:

- a deck of cards, well shuffled
- two pieces of paper, one marked *CORRECT*, the other marked *INCORRECT*
- a pen or pencil
- two people, one to send and the other to receive telepathic messages

1. The sender sits at a table, lays out the two pieces of paper and places the cards face down in a pile. The receiver sits at the other side of the table, facing away from the sender. This is important, because the receiver must not be able to see the cards.

2. The sender picks up a card and concentrates on its colour. The receiver tries to identify its colour and says out loud either red or black.

3. If the receiver correctly identifies the colour of the card, the sender places it on the paper marked *CORRECT*. If not, it goes on the paper marked *INCORRECT*.

4. Do this for nine more cards then record how many out of the first batch of ten were correct.

5. Do four more batches of cards. Reshuffle the pack, then do five more batches, for a total of 100 cards. Add up the total score.

If you did nothing but guess the colour of 100 cards, the odds are that you would accurately identify between 40 and 60 of them. If, however, you accurately identified more than 60 of them, something other than guesswork might be taking place. Is it ESP? Your guess is as good as anyone's!

Haven't We Met Before?

A random telephone poll of 1,236 adults in the U.S. conducted in 1991 by the *Skeptical Inquirer* revealed that a surprising number of them believe in supernatural phenomena. If you attended a party with 100 of the Americans polled, you'd meet 25 people who believe in ghosts, 10 who claim to have been in the presence of a ghost and 25 who say they have communicated telepathically with another person. And at least half of them believe in ESP.

OUT OF THIS WORLD

Look through the history books and you'll find reports of unidentified flying objects (UFOs) in the sky going back hundreds of years. Are we any closer to solving the mystery of UFOs now than people were then?

Could aliens from another part of our galaxy have been dropping by Earth to visit for the last 2,000 years? How likely is it that life exists outside our solar system anyhow? Are UFOs evidence of extra-terrestrial intelligence or are they something just as weird from this planet?

And what about the remarkably similar reports from people who claim to have been abducted by aliens? Surely people can recognize when their brains are playing tricks on them. Or can they?

If you're going to spend time searching the sky for UFOs, you might be better off keeping an eye out for asteroids. If anything alien is going to land on Earth during the next century, it's more likely to be an asteroid than a spaceship! So strap yourself in, it's time to blast off for a little space travel . . .

UFO Alert

The afternoon of June 24, 1947, was bright and clear. Pilot Kenneth Arnold had just begun his aerial search for an aircraft that had gone down in the Cascade Mountains near Seattle, Washington. Suddenly a bluish-white flash lit up the sky. And another. Then Arnold was amazed to see nine silver aircraft, each with a wingspan of about 30 m (33 yards). Using familiar landmarks as reference, Arnold estimated that they were flying at least 1,930 km/h (1,200 mph) – twice the speed of most aircraft in 1947!

Thinking he might have witnessed some kind of secret weapon, Arnold reported his sighting to the authorities. He described the aircraft as flying through the air like a saucer might skip across water. The next day, headlines proclaimed: "Flying Saucers!"

If not alien spacecraft, what did Kenneth Arnold see? One possibility is that he witnessed "earth lights," sometimes seen in areas where faults in the earth's crust cause rock surfaces to grind together. The stress produced in the rocks by grinding movements is thought to create bright flashes of light. An American geologist, who has duplicated these intense flashes of light in his laboratory by stressing rocks until they broke apart, suggested that naturally created earth lights might move along the line of an active fault. So both the flashes and the high-speed silvery "saucers" could have come from faults in the earth's crust beneath the Cascade Mountains.

Dancing Carrots

An atmospheric scientist in Fort Collins, Colorado, filmed carrots dancing 80 km (50 miles) above thunderstorm clouds. That's how he described mysterious orange columns and blobs of light in the upper atmosphere. Scientists at the University of Alaska have also seen dancing carrots, but these looked more like red jellyfish trailing tentacles. And that's not all. ELVES — flickering discs of green lightning — have been detected on the fringes of space. Like their namesakes, these ELVES (Emissions of Light and Very low frequency perturbations due to Electromagnetic pulse Sources) can't be seen by the human eye. So far, carrots, jellyfish and ELVES all remain unsolved mysteries.

Arnold wasn't the first person to see a UFO, or Unidentified Flying Object. There had been reports of strange lights in the sky for centuries. In 776, during a battle between the Saxons and the Franks, fiery UFOs in the shape of military shields appeared in the sky. And in 1561 in Nuremberg, Germany, people reported seeing large "tubes" in the sky from which discs emerged and appeared to "fight" with each other. Kenneth Arnold's sighting was only one of thousands, but it was the one that started the flying saucer craze of the 1950s. And many people took UFOs very seriously. From 1952 to 1969, the U.S. Air Force carried out an official investigation into UFOs, known as Project Blue Book. And the Canadian government set up a UFO investigation agency called Project Magnet.

The Friendly Skies?

On January 6, 1995, something caused the flight crew of a British Airways Boeing 737 to duck. Hurtling towards them was a brightly-lit wedge-shaped object, passing close enough to "buzz" the plane. After a year-long inquiry into the UFO, British aviation experts admitted they couldn't find a logical explanation for it. Even more baffling — although the UFO was also seen from the ground, it didn't show up on any radar screens.

UFOs to IFOs

An Unidentified Flying Object is anything seen in the sky that cannot be identified. According to one UFO researcher, a UFO sighting occurs somewhere on Earth every three minutes.

Researchers have often been able to turn UFOs into identified flying objects, or IFOs. There are natural phenomena that can easily be taken for alien spacecraft. These include weather balloons reflecting sunlight and sightings of very bright celestial bodies like the planet Venus. Strangely shaped clouds – like the lenticular, or lens-shaped, clouds sometimes found near mountains – can look like flying saucers.

Another natural phenomenon frequently mistaken for a UFO is Sirius, the "dog star." Each spring a certain Canadian astronomer receives phone calls from people describing a flashing light that changes from red to blue to green in the southwest around 10 o'clock at night. It's Sirius, low on the horizon. The thick, rippling blanket of atmosphere breaks up its light, changing its colour and making it appear to flash. The dog star certainly causes a lot of barking each spring!

The **X**-Files?

J ust one week after Kenneth Arnold's encounter with
"flying saucers" over the Cascade Mountains, a huge
explosion was heard during a thunderstorm near the
town of Roswell, New Mexico. When a ranch manager
named Brazel checked on his sheep the next morning,
he found what appeared to be the scattered remains of
some kind of aircraft. But the pieces were made of some
strange material he'd never seen before. And they were
covered in strange designs that made no sense to him.

Brazel took samples of the material to the sheriff in
Roswell, who notified the U.S. Air Force. Air Force
investigators quickly sealed off the site. The official Air
Force explanation was that the debris was from a
downed weather balloon.

It wasn't long, however, before a rumour began to
circulate that the bodies of four extra-terrestrial aliens
had been found near the crash site. The story spread
that the aliens had ejected before their craft exploded.
The rumour gathered strength when a military witness
claimed that he had flown the bodies of the aliens out of
Roswell in crates. Was the U.S. Air Force trying to cover
up the truth about what it had found?

People have been arguing about the Roswell incident
ever since. Finally, in 1994, the U.S. Air Force issued
another official statement saying that it is not hiding an
alien spaceship, or the bodies of its crew. What the Air
Force was trying to cover up in 1947, they said, was the

explosion of a top-secret Pentagon balloon, designed to detect sound waves produced by enemy nuclear explosions. Meanwhile, no one at the UFO Museum at Roswell believes a word of it.

The Circle Game

In the 1980s and early 1990s, a bumper crop of mysterious circles grew in farmers' fields in the south of England (see photo) and other places worldwide. Could the circles and geometric patterns have been made by the landing gear of visiting spacecraft? In 1991, the hopes of UFO enthusiasts were dashed when Douglas Bower and David Chorley confessed that they had made many of the English circles since 1978. And in Japan, high school students claimed responsibility for crop circles in a rice paddy. But then who made the circles in Canada, the U.S., France and other places around the world?

Photo Fakes

There have been hundreds of attempts over the years to pass off faked photographs of UFOs as the genuine item. Below is a photograph of a UFO. Is it a fake? *Answer on page 100.*

Of course, now computers can alter and add to photographs so well that it's impossible to tell that they've been faked. Chances are no one will believe UFO photographs ever again!

Don't Try This At Home

The fuzzy black and white photo (above) of a single UFO was part of a joke that got out of hand. Fifteen-year-old Dan Jaroslaw made a model of a flying saucer. He and his brother Grant strung it up on clear thread between two poles, and they took four Polaroid photos of it. The joke backfired when their mother saw the photos and called the newspapers. For the next nine years the photographs were considered by experts to be classic examples of a daylight UFO appearance. Finally, in 1976 the embarrassed Jaroslaw brothers admitted that the photos were fake. Keep this story in mind if you're thinking of faking some UFO photos of your own!

Too CLOSE for Comfort

A well-known psychologist from Harvard University has worked closely with people who claim to have been abducted by aliens. He's confident that his patients are not suffering from mental illness, and their obvious distress has convinced him that something really did happen to them.

Many abductees report waking up, often to a bright light. They sense a presence in the room. Sometimes it holds them down and they're unable to move. To many psychologists this sounds like a good description of sleep paralysis. When you're fast asleep and dreaming, your muscles become paralyzed so that you don't hurt yourself by acting out your dreams. But sometimes your brain messes up and you become paralyzed while you're awake. It can happen to exhausted or stressed-out drivers, and bright lights sometimes trigger it. It's thought that as many as a quarter of all people have suffered from sleep paralysis while awake. And the vast majority of them sensed a presence near them.

Many cultures have legends of beings that sit on a sleeping person's chest and keep the sleeper from moving or breathing. They are probably created to explain sleep paralysis. But even if sleep paralysis seems to account for many of the things abductees experience, it doesn't explain why they feel as if they are floating into a spaceship and being touched by aliens. We have to look further for an explanation for these sensations.

Close Encounters of the Scary Kind

At first, people reported seeing UFOs at close range (close encounters of the first kind), or finding evidence like burn marks on the ground following a UFO sighting (close encounters of the second kind). Soon people claimed to have made contact with aliens (close encounters of the third kind) and eventually reported being abducted by aliens (close encounters of the fourth and scariest kind).

All Wired Up

A neurobiologist at Laurentian University in Sudbury, Ontario, thinks that abductees' experiences of floating and being touched could all take place in their heads. He believes that these feelings are hallucinations brought on by unusual bursts of electrical activity in the temporal lobes of the brain – the part of your brain just above your ears. To prove his theory he tried to create the feelings in a volunteer in his laboratory.

He fitted a motorcycle helmet with solenoids – coils of wire that create magnetic fields when electricity is passed through them. Next, he used a computer to copy the unusual pattern of electrical activity that produces a floating sensation. Then, he sent this pattern through the solenoids into the volunteer's brain, triggering the same bursts of electrical activity in her temporal lobes.

The volunteer first felt as if she were swaying in a hammock, then as if two hands grabbed her shoulders and pulled her body up out of the chair. Of course, she was hallucinating – she was still sitting and no one had touched her. Next, she felt as if her leg were being stretched halfway up the wall to the ceiling. People with very active temporal lobes are thought to have these kinds of hallucinations most often while they sleep. Can you imagine how frightening it must be to wake up feeling that you're floating and being touched by unknown beings?

Goblins or Aliens

The details of most UFO abduction stories are remarkably similar: lots of strange lights; small aliens with large heads, enormous eyes and thin, spindly arms and legs. The picture above is a hoax, but the features match most descriptions by people who claim to have seen extra-terrestrial beings. Usually they wear pale, close-fitting clothes and carry humans away in the night. Sound familiar? Creatures like this have been populating our stories for centuries — as goblins, elves, fairies, leprechauns, and bogeymen! Are aliens really elves with a fancy set of wheels?

Is ANYONE Out There?

If we want to find other life in our galaxy, what should we be looking for? To begin with, astronomers think that since the Sun, a G-class star, produced just the right climate for life on one of its planets, other G-class stars could do the same. Second, we should look for an element essential to life as we know it – water. In our solar system, there is a narrow zone where water can exist as a liquid. Too close to the sun and it evaporates, too far away and it freezes. Luckily for us, Earth orbits in this zone.

One Crazy Planet

What's too hot to handle, as big as Jupiter and orbiting a star called 51 Pegasus once every four days? If Swiss astronomers are correct, it's the first planet outside our own solar system to be discovered orbiting a star that's the same type as our Sun. This is exciting news, but some things don't add up. To complete an orbit in only four days, the planet must be so close to 51 Pegasus that it practically skims its surface. According to current theories, it's impossible for a planet the size of Jupiter to do this. Are the theories off base? Or should the Swiss astronomers pull out their calculators again?

Late in 1995, Swiss astronomers proved that G-class stars were good places to look for planets. Three months later, American astronomers confirmed the Swiss discovery. Then they announced their own discovery of two huge planets orbiting Sun-type stars: one in the constellation Virgo, the other in Ursa Major, the Plough. And both planets orbit in a zone that supports water.

Infrared pictures of at least one of the planets have been captured by the Hubble Space Telescope. Meanwhile, Europe's Infrared Space Observatory (ISO) satellite continues its search for more planets. NASA hopes to build a new generation of space telescopes for a clear look at what it hopes will be many distant new worlds.

Some scientists are pretty sure that Earth is not the only planet with life on it. Others are not. Scientists use different formulas to work out how many planets might support life, or if that life could be intelligent and able to communicate. Here's one way of figuring out the odds.

1. Assume there are 400 billion stars in the Milky Way Galaxy.
2. Assume one-tenth of them, or 40 billion, have planets.
3. An average of 10 planets to a star makes 400 billion planets.
4. If only one planet of the ten orbiting each star is in the right climate zone (like Earth in our solar system), that makes 40 billion planets that can support life.
5. Assume that life has evolved on one-tenth of them, or 4 billion planets.

6. If only one-hundredth of those planets have intelligent life, that makes 40 million civilizations in our galaxy.
7. If only one-tenth of these civilizations have developed radio technology, that makes 4 million civilizations able to send messages into space. (However, one scientist suggests that many of them could not have developed radio technology because their planets are probably missing vital metals.)
8. The universe is so old that many civilizations would have come and gone by now. If only one-thousandth of them are at the right stage in their development, *that means there could be 4,000 civilizations out there ready to communicate!*

Of course, other formulas end up concluding that there is only one planet with life on it . . . and you're on it!

It Came from Outer Space

We should be keeping an eye on the sky, but not just for alien spacecraft. On June 30, 1908, something exploded in the sky near the Tunguska River in Siberia with the force of a 20 megaton nuclear bomb. It flattened and burned trees covering an area almost as big as New York City.

Tunguska had a visitor from space. Scientists wondered if it was a lump of antimatter, a miniature black hole, or even something called a "puffball" comet. The fact that it lacked a crater and the pattern of damage done to the trees – all radiating out from a central spot like gigantic, charred toothpicks – confirms that whatever exploded did so in the air.

What's the most likely space object to leave the kind of evidence found at Tunguska? According to a computer simulation done by NASA researchers in 1993, it's a stony asteroid about the size of two side-by-side ice hockey rinks, travelling at 15 km/sec (33,480 mph). An asteroid of this size and speed would break up about 8 km (5 miles) above the ground. That's the point where the difference in pressure between the air piling up in front of the asteroid and the near-vacuum created behind it becomes too much for it to withstand.

The asteroid that did so much damage at Tunguska was relatively small. What would happen if a really big asteroid or comet hit the earth? Well, 65 million years ago something enormous smashed into Mexico's Yucatan Peninsula. It left a crater that would almost cover the distance between London and Paris, released as much energy as 200 million hydrogen bombs and kicked up a cloud of dust that blocked the sun for months. Some scientists also believe that a firestorm consumed at least a quarter of the world's plants. When the sun finally shone again, many species, including the dinosaurs, were dead.

Near Miss

Two weeks before Christmas in 1994 an asteroid measuring 6 to 13 m (6.5 – 14 yards) across whizzed past the earth 104,000 km (65,000 miles) away. That's not as far away as it sounds — only about one quarter of the distance between here and the moon. As many as ten stony asteroids this size are probably burned up in Earth's atmosphere every year.

Death by Asteroid?

Don't worry. Our planet's atmosphere burns up small chunks of incoming space debris and its gravity causes many asteroids to speed up, change their orbit and avoid collision. However, NASA experts have suggested that a network of telescopes should be established around the world to hunt down Earth-bound asteroids that might cause problems. And people are already

working out what we should do if someone does spot an incoming asteroid one day. There has been talk of nudging it back out to space with a very powerful nuclear weapon. Where's Superman when you need him?

Guardian Planet

Next time you see the giant gas planet Jupiter in the evening sky, say a quiet thank you to it. Its gravity acts on comets that are headed towards Earth, sending them veering off in another direction. Without our guardian planet, Jupiter, it's likely that Earth would have been involved in a major space collision — of the size that destroyed the dinosaurs — once every 100,000 years instead of once every 100 million years.

Breaking Away

It's thought that an asteroid the size of the planet Mars collided with Earth about 4 billion years ago, making it spin faster on its axis. The debris, flung into orbit by the explosion, slowly joined together, forming a rocky satellite we later called the Moon

Star Nursery

During the winter you can see a nursery in the sky where stars are being born. And the Hubble Space Telescope has confirmed that these newborn stars are surrounded by glowing discs of dust and gas – the stuff that planets are made of. Our Sun would have looked like one of these stars about 5 billion years ago, and our planet would have been part of the glowing disc around it.

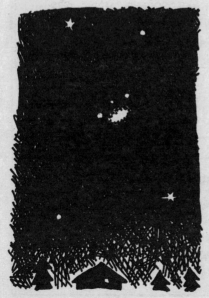

To see this star nursery for yourself, choose a clear, moonless winter night. If you live in a city, try to get away from sources of light. Look south to find the constellation of Orion (see illustration at left), then find the fuzzy white patch below Orion's belt. Through binoculars you can see that it's the bowl-shaped Orion Nebula – a vast nursery of

newborn stars in the process of making
planets. Its white glow comes from the very
bright stars, called the Trapezium, clustered at
its centre.

Stargazing Hint

You'll see the nebula much better if you
look slightly off to one side of it. This
will allow the rod cells around the
edges of your vision to pick up its light. They're better at
seeing things in dim light than the cone cells at the
centre of your vision. Astronomers call this
using averted vision, and they do it all the
time.

Amazing But True

The Hubble Space Telescope reveals thousands of galaxies
near the Plough's handle. Astronomers estimate the
number of galaxies in the visible universe to be a
staggering 40 billion!

Larger **THAN LIFE**

On April 1, 1995, the discovery of a strange new animal was reported in a popular science magazine. The Hotheaded Naked Ice Borer was said to lurk beneath the ice in Antarctica, hunting penguins by melting the ice they stood on and pulling them into the slush. A photograph showed a pincer-toothed monster with a hot red bump on its forehead. But anyone asking for concrete proof of the Ice Borer's existence was in for a major disappointment. It was all a colossal hoax, an April Fool's joke.

Cryptozoologists are people who spend their lives searching for mysterious animals. And they've found proof that, unlike the Ice Borer, some strange, hidden beasts are real. Giant pandas gave hunters and zoo collectors the slip for more than 50 years, until a baby panda was caught napping in a tree in northern China in 1937. And as for the gorilla, the more the rumours flew, the bigger and more ferocious it loomed in people's minds. Then in the 19th century, it was proved that the huge, hairy gorilla was no myth. Like pandas and gorillas, creatures like Bigfoot, Yeti and the Loch Ness Monster are said to live in remote places. And if we haven't captured them so far, does that mean they don't exist?

Ancient tales are full of heroes battling fabulous beasts like gryphons or fire-breathing dragons. Legendary or real, monsters have fascinated humans for a long time. Ready to step into some big footprints and get to the murky bottom of some monstrous tales?

. . . And Twice as UGLY

It's called Sasquatch, although many people prefer its laid-back California name of Bigfoot. No matter what you call it, it's a huge, cone-headed, hairy creature that lumbers along on two feet and lives in the rugged mountains along the Pacific coast of North America. What is there to prove that Bigfoot exists? Nothing that scientists accept as firm evidence – no skeleton, not even a skull. Is it any wonder most scientists won't take Bigfoot seriously? All they have to go on is some "soft" evidence: a few sightings, lots of footprints and a short film.

Did You Know?

Sasquatch, derived from a word used by the Salish tribe of southwest British Columbia, means "wild man of the woods."

There seem to be two different types of Bigfoot prints. Some look as if they've been left by gigantic humans, like the print found at Bossburg in Washington State. The plaster cast of the print is almost 44 cm (17 inches) long, which would make its owner almost 3 m (9.5 feet) tall! Other footprints don't look like giant humans left them. They are roughly hourglass-shaped like the footprint found on Blue Creek Mountain in northern California. (Pictures on page 84.)

Scientists find it suspicious that two distinct kinds of

15 inch Bigfoot track found on Blue Creek Moutain, California, in September 1967

prints are found, because it's unlikely that two different species of Bigfoot would evolve and survive in the same area. One expert on how primates walk thinks this means at least one type of footprint must be fake. And many Bigfoot prints

have already been exposed as fakes. It doesn't take an expert long to recognize whether a footprint has been made by a moving, weight-bearing foot or has been stamped out by a pair of footprint-shaped boots! (Discover these differences yourself by doing the activity on page 97.)

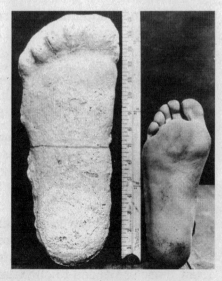

A man's foot (above right) compared with a cast of a Bigfoot footprint (found in Bluff Creek, northern California, USA, after the sighting and filming of Bigfoot by Roger Patterson in 1967).

Lights! Camera! . . . Action?

Roger Patterson's short film, taken in 1967 in Bluff Creek Valley, should have provided definite proof of Bigfoot's existence. But most scientists who have seen the film think that its "star" is probably a man in a fur suit. The film shows a female Bigfoot walking with exaggerated strides into the forest. At one point, shown in the frame on page 86, she turns and looks at the camera. Scientists raised the following questions after seeing the film and checking the footprints the subject of the film left behind.

- If it's female, why does this Bigfoot move like a male?

- Why is she walking in such a self-conscious, exaggerated way?

- Why is she apelike above the waist and humanlike below? This half-and-half mix is never seen in nature.

- Why does her head have a bony crest? In the large primates, like orangutans and gorillas, head crests are normally seen only on males.

- Why doesn't she have a pot belly, which normally goes with a bony crest? (A crest anchors the extra jaw muscles needed to chew large quantities of low-energy food, which creates a pot belly as it's being processed.)

- If, as one expert deduced, she is 196 cm (6.4 feet) tall, why are her footprints those of a creature much taller than this?

- Why is the space between each footprint shorter than the distance the size of the footprint demands?

An expert in how humans move felt that knowing the exact speed at which the film was shot could help him determine whether the Bigfoot was real or fake. If the movie had been shot at 24 frames per second (fps) then the Bigfoot could be a large man in a hairy suit. But if the film had been shot at 18 fps, the way the Bigfoot was moving was not the way a human would walk.

Patterson said that he couldn't remember what speed he was shooting at that day. All these questions strongly suggest that either the footprints were faked or the film was. And if one was faked, how can we believe either?

That There THING

I n 1952, Tensing Norgay, a Sherpa tribesman and skilled mountain guide, was one of the first people to reach the top of Mount Everest on the border between Nepal and Tibet. A reporter asked him whether the Yeti – the Asian equivalents to Bigfoot – were real.

Tensing Norgay preferred to think of Yeti as bogeymen conjured up by mums to scare naughty kids into behaving. Is there evidence to prove they're real?

A number of alleged Yeti tracks have been photographed on the snowy slopes of the Himalayan mountains, none of them the same. One of the clearest photos (right) was taken in 1951 by mountaineer Eric Shipton when he came across a set of tracks at a height of 6,000 m (19,685 feet). The ice axe gives an idea of the size of the footprint. It is almost 33 cm (13 inches) long and 20 cm (8 inches) wide.

This photo caused a stir. The deep impression around the outer edge of the heel suggested that whatever made it walked like a human being, with the outer side of the heel striking the ground first. But a closer look revealed that the snow had been exposed to sunlight and the deep heel print was likely to have been caused by melting. The print was probably made by an animal, but what kind? Eventually, one footprint expert came up with an interesting theory. Perhaps the print was a combination of two footprints. Red bears live in the Himalayas. When bears move quickly their footprints can overlap. This expert also had another, even more interesting explanation for the footprint – that it belonged to a human being. Why would anyone stroll barefoot through the snow? Incredibly, pilgrims sometimes travel barefoot through the mountains on their way to sacred sites.

A Gigantic Possibility

In an expedition to Nepal in 1959, a cryptozoologist discovered what he thought were Yeti droppings. They contained an unknown type of parasitic worm. Since each species of mammal has its own parasites, the droppings might have come from an equally unknown animal. What might it be?

An anthropologist at Washington State University thinks that if Yeti and Bigfoot do exist, they might descend from a giant apelike creature known as

Gigantopithecus, which became extinct 300,000 years ago. Scientists have discovered three fossilized jawbones, larger than the jawbones of male gorillas, and some teeth from Gigantopithecus. Some of these fossils were discovered in the foothills of the Himalayas, near where Yeti are supposed to live. Unfortunately, jawbones can't tell us for certain whether Gigantopithecus walked upright. And a large jawbone doesn't guarantee that its owner was tall. The jawbone of a male gorilla is much larger than the jawbone of a man of the same height.

So what does the evidence show? Not enough. Most scientists are not convinced that Yeti and Bigfoot are anything more than mythical beasts, even if the myths might have been based on creatures that once lived. Scientists need the living creatures or their bones to examine before they can be satisfied that Sasquatch and Yeti still roam the mountains today.

A Handy Tale

A skeletal hand, supposedly a Yeti's, was kept by Buddhist monks at their monastery in Pangboche. Decades ago, a few bones and a piece of shrivelled skin from the Pangboche hand were smuggled out of Nepal to be tested in the U.S. The results of the analysis were finally released, 30 years later, in February 1992. They revealed that although the skin from the hand was similar to human skin, it wasn't quite human. Unfortunately, further research into the Pangboche hand is now out of the question. It was stolen from the monastery in 1991.

Who's Alma?

An Alma is a mystery creature of the Caucasus Mountains in Central Asia. Compared with Bigfoot and Yeti, however, Almas have been downright friendly with humans. According to some eyewitness reports, they even try to communicate with gestures. Some scientists think that if Almas are real, there is a faint possibility they might have descended from the Neanderthals — one of our ancient ancestors — that are known to have lived in this region as recently as 30,000 years ago. A joint Russian-French expedition into the area in 1992 failed to confirm the existence of Almas. All the team came home with were footprints, droppings and stories. Sound familiar?

Searching for NESSIE

Tim Dinsdale, an English engineer, spent months watching the waters of Scotland's Loch Ness in 1960. One afternoon his patience was rewarded when he filmed what he thought was the legendary Loch Ness Monster, or Nessie for short. Dinsdale's film showed a large, hump-backed object moving across the loch at about 16 km/h (10 mph). Dinsdale's film was too grainy and was taken too far away to make a positive identification. It did, however, spark a flurry of Nessie-hunting activity.

Loch Ness is a long, narrow ribbon of a lake that's deeper than the North Sea. Its waters are murky, full of dark brown particles of peat – very soft coal – that get washed into the loch from surrounding bogs. All the dark particles in the water make underwater photography extremely difficult. Divers say the loch is frightening because its water is so black. Finding Nessie under these circumstances calls for unusual techniques.

First, scientists from Cambridge University bounced echo-sounding beams off the bottom of the loch. They thought the beams would annoy living creatures so much that they would surface. Sure enough, up popped some very grouchy salmon. Next, another group thought that explosions might wake up Nessie. Out came the dynamite and in 1963 eyewitnesses recorded 40 sightings of Nessie, who by now must have been only one of many extremely annoyed loch residents. In 1968, engineers from the University of Birmingham bounced sound off underwater objects moving at high speed. We never discovered what the objects were because people found reasons to doubt the recordings, and so the evidence was ignored.

Fooled You!

The Loch Ness Monster seems to attract as many hoaxers as it does searchers. The picture below is probably the most famous Nessie photo of all time. It was taken on April 1, 1934, by R.K. Wilson, a doctor from London. The date says it all. And then Sir Peter Scott decided Nessie needed a proper scientific name. He suggested: *Nessiteras rhombopteryx*.

Only later was it discovered that the name was a joke. Can you rearrange the letters in the name to find out Sir Peter's message?

Answer on page 100.

A research team from the Academy of Applied Sciences in Boston took underwater photos in Loch Ness in 1972, and sent them to NASA for computer enhancement. One photo showed a large flipper joined to a large body. Three years later, the same process produced two more photos. Surely this time scientists had firm evidence of Nessie's existence? Sorry! People were concerned that the computer enhancement could distort the photos so that they looked more like what we wanted to see than what they actually are.

What's in the Loch?

The search for Nessie continues. Several highly respected scientists feel the evidence suggests that large aquatic animals do live in Loch Ness. What kind of animals might they be?

The suggestions range from eels and turtles to prehistoric creatures called plesiosaurs. Most sightings describe Nessie with the same features: a small snakelike head, a long slim neck, a heavy body, a long powerful tail, one to three humps and four diamond-shaped fins. The photos that haven't yet proved to be hoaxes seem to confirm this description. The animal that best fits this description of Nessie is the plesiosaur. What are the chances a creature believed extinct for millions of years didn't die out altogether? Could a few ancient animals have hidden in the depths of Loch Ness? The mystery of Loch Ness is far from over. And as far as scientists are concerned, only the capture of a living Nessie or the discovery of its bones will solve the mystery for good.

Extinct Fish Found Alive!

In 1938 a fisherman hauled
in his net off the east coast of Africa
and discovered he'd caught a fish that officially
didn't exist. It was a coelacanth, which scientists
thought had become extinct
70 million years ago.

Mythical MONSTERS

Ancient legends tell of heroic battles fought against
terrifying monsters: the gryphon that guards its
treasure and the dragon, superstar of mythical
beasts. How did these legends begin?

Terror Bird or Dinosaur?

The gryphon, with the head of an eagle and the body of
a lion, has a weakness for precious metals and stones. If
anyone gets too close to its treasure, it pounces on them
and tears them to pieces.

How did people dream up such a creature? One idea is
that the gryphon is based on a prehistoric flightless bird,
known as Titanis. Standing taller than an elephant and
able to outrun a horse, Titanis belonged to a group of
fierce predators known as terror birds. Humans, who
evolved near the end of the terror birds'
reign, must have had some awesome
fireside tales to tell about
encounters with Titanis. Its
treasure, of course, would be its
nest full of eggs or young that it
had to protect from marauding
mammals.

Another explanation is
linked to the
possibility that

ancient nomads from a region north of the Black Sea might have come across the fossilized remains of the dinosaur *Protoceratops* while travelling in Mongolia. This horned dinosaur had a skull that looks a bit like a giant eagle head, and feet that look more at home on a lion than on a dinosaur. If the confused nomads also discovered fossilized dinosaur eggs, it could explain why the gryphon supposedly laid eggs as hard as stone!

Birds of a Feather

Prehistoric Titanis makes it easy to believe that birds are the direct descendants of small, meat-eating dinosaurs. And the seriema bird, a living relative of terror birds, is still found in the grasslands of South America. It hunts prey just like its ancestors did – at racehorse speed! But don't worry – it's only slightly taller than a chicken.

There be Dragons . . .

There's hardly a place in the world that doesn't have a dragon in its mythology. Could the dragon, like the gryphon, be based on a real-life animal that once terrorized us? If so, what animal might that be? The dinosaur springs immediately to mind, but dinosaurs couldn't have inspired people to believe in dragons. Even if some dinosaurs managed to survive for a few million years after most of them disappeared, there's still a gap of tens of millions of years before people came along. So dragons couldn't be based on actual sightings by people of living dinosaurs.

It's possible that people discovered the fossilized bones of dinosaurs, and based the dragon on them. Back then, the bones wouldn't have provided specific clues to what the beast looked like, so where did the details come from? The dragon brings us back to where we started in this book . . . back to our ancient fears of being hunted and of creatures of the night. Look closely at dragons and you'll see that they're made up of bits and pieces of animals we love to hate. A dragon's long, scaly body can only have come from a snake. Indeed, many dragons have no legs, and our word dragon comes from the Greek word *dracon*, which means serpent or snake. Its head looks like a cross between the head of a crocodile and the head of a wolf. Major fangs! Its feet resemble those of a large bird of prey, perhaps even those of Titanis. While its skin-covered wings, if it's got them, look as if they come from an enormous bat.

No wonder the dragon is such a mega-monster. We've endowed it with the powers of animals that have paralyzed us with fear for longer than anyone can remember.

Living Dragons

A Dutch plane crash-landed in 1912 on the island of Komodo in Indonesia. What the pilot reported seeing made headline news: huge, dragonlike creatures that sometimes attacked and ate people.

Scientists investigated the report. They confirmed that what the pilot saw were giant monitor lizards — reptiles that can be more than 3 m (10 feet) in length. Unconfirmed reports of even larger lizards have come out of New Guinea. Could sightings of these giant lizards by our ancestors have inspired the dragon of mythology?

Make TRACKS

How can human
footprints look like
Bigfoot-prints?

. . . In the Snow

To find out you'll need:
- a patch of snow
  that gets sunshine
  most of the day
- a piece of thick cardboard and a
  cardboard box
- scissors, a ruler, paper and pencil

1. Make a cardboard cutout of your right footprint (do a
   barefoot trace) and make two footprints with it 3 cm
   (about 1 inch) deep in the snow.
2. Record their length, greatest width and heel width.
3. Cover one with the box, making sure that the box
   doesn't shade the other one.
4. Measure the prints morning and afternoon for about
   four days.
   What happens to them both?

. . . In the Sand

How can you tell a walking footprint from a stamped
impression of a footprint? Walk barefoot through mud

or wet sand. Then hop a couple of steps before pressing your raised foot firmly into the sand beside your supporting foot. Try to bring it straight down so that all points on the bottom of your foot touch the sand at the same time. You're pretending that your foot is a plaster cast and you're stamping its impression into the sand. Compare this standing print with one of your walking prints. What are the differences?

Answer on page 100.

A Scientific Secret

You can figure out how tall a person – or a Bigfoot – is by a footprint. Simply measure the length of a print then multiply this figure by 6.6 to give you the height of whoever made it.

Answers

1, A; 2, D; 3, B; 4, C.

Spot the Phobia, page 11-12
1, J; 2, G; 3, A; 4, H; 5, D; 6, I; 7, F; 8, B; 9, E; 10, C.

Who's Superstitious Here?, pages 17-20

1, C. Salt is the substance considered so important that it was bad luck to spill it. Spilled salt is thrown over the left side of the body. That's the side controlled by the right side of the brain, which is thought to handle negative emotions. Might this relate to the notion that left stands for evil, right stands for good?

2, H. Knocking on wood with the right hand – controlled by the left side of your brain, responsible for positive emotions – supposedly keeps you from harm when you're talking too big.

3, D. It's widely thought to be bad luck when a black cat crosses your path. Cats have been seen as special animals ever since the Egyptians worshipped them as gods.

4, F. Breaking a mirror is believed to be bad luck. To offset the bad luck, you must gather all the pieces and throw them into a fast-flowing stream or river. The Romans who set the bad luck at seven years were on the right track: your bones renew themselves completely every seven years.

5, J. The number 13 is considered to be an unlucky number. Science fiction writer H.G. Wells thought that the superstitions about 13 developed because it's awkward – unlike the number 12, it can't be divided evenly.

6, A. Walking under a ladder is thought to be bad luck. One possible source for this superstition was a type of gallows that was propped against a supporting beam, like a ladder. The condemned criminal who was about to be hanged on this type of gallows could escape by climbing up to reach the rope!

7, E. Saying "Bless you" to someone who sneezes is supposed to bring good luck to the sneezer.

8, G. If you tie a string around your finger, it's thought that seeing it will help you remember something. And as a bonus, the knot is supposed to ward off evil.

9, I. Stirring food counterclockwise would be considered good luck for sun-worshippers. Stirring clockwise, on the other hand, is considered bad luck and means the food won't taste right.

10, B. If you step on pavement cracks, it is thought to bring bad luck to your family. A poem is most likely the source of our modern superstition:
Step in a hole, and you'll break your mother's sugar bowl.
Step on a crack, and you'll break your mother's back.

Step in a ditch, and your mother's nose will itch.
Step on the dirt, and you'll tear your father's shirt.
Step on a nail, and you'll put your father in jail.

Full Moon Madness, pp 40-41

You've probably figured out by now that the moon doesn't change size as it travels across the sky. It's all an optical illusion. The experiments with the pill and paper tube prove that. A pill held at arm's length always exactly covers the moon, and the moon always fills the end of the tube – both on the horizon and high in the sky. But how did you make the moon shrink by looking at it through your legs? You did it by removing the horizon from your view.

Your brain contains maps of the space around you – ranging from the space immediately surrounding you to the space all the way out to the horizon – to keep you aware of your position in relation to other things. But your brain's big space map is warped. On it, the horizon appears farther away than a point on the sky directly overhead. So when the moon at the horizon makes the same size image on the retina of your eyes as the moon overhead, your brain has to explain why something that is supposed to be farther away can still be the same size as something closer. So it fools you into thinking the moon is bigger at the horizon than it actually is!

Animals Do the Strangest Things, pp 56-57

Animals do all of these things in the hours leading up to an earthquake.

Losing Your Marbles, page 59

This question was adapted from one used in experiments at the University of the West of England.

The answer: blue. There are 10 marbles left; 8 of them are blue and 2 are red. The odds are 4 to 1 in favour, therefore, of you picking a blue one next time.

Photo Fakes, page 69

The photo is a fake, made in the early 1990s. As photo alteration techniques got more sophisticated, effects like shadows and differences in focus could be faked quite accurately.

Fooled You! page 92

Nessiteras rhombopteryx can be unscrambled to read "Monster hoax by Sir Peter S."

Make Tracks, page 97

When you walk, you usually strike the ground with the outside of your heel and push off from the ground with your big toe. The result is that your walking footprint is deeper along the outside edge of the heel. Also, you walk with your feet slightly turned out at the toes – it's known as your angle of gait. If you come across footprints in the sand that have no deeper indentation on the outside of the heel and are pointing straight ahead, you'll know immediately they're faked!

Spooky Scientists — A Glossary

Here are some of the researchers whose work helps uncover the truth behind many bizarre mysteries.

Anthropologists study how human beings evolved. They're big on studying bones ancient and new. They also try to find clues about how we lived our lives before anyone kept a record of history.

Astronomers are spacy people. They look through telescopes and compare photographs and other records of stars, planets, moons, comets and galaxies – all in an attempt to understand how the universe works.

Astrophysicists are astronomers who ask questions such as *what are stars and planets made of?*, *how are stars born?*, and *why do stars die?*

Atmospheric scientists aren't airheads, but they are fascinated by the gaseous envelope that surrounds our planet, called the atmosphere – its makeup, the way it acts, and all the mysterious things that go on in it.

Biochemists just love figuring out what living things are made of – all the chemical combinations and reactions that go on in our bodies, and in lots of other bodies too.

Biologists need to know how living things work – how they got to be the way they are, live the places they live and get along with other living things.

Chemists are into substances. They study elements and how they combine to form compounds. **Physical chemists** work out how the physical properties of substances affect the way they combine and change.

Cryptozoologists trek around in hard-to-reach places, searching high and low for mysterious animals that few people believe exist.

Doctors, dentists and **nutritionists** not only keep us healthy, but often explore the way our bodies work to figure out the best ways to do their jobs.

Engineers apply science to structures and machines, designing and building them, and making them work. **Aviation experts** and **rocket scientists** are engineers who specialize in making things work way out there in the sky and beyond.

Geneticists float around in gene pools, studying the characteristics that are determined from birth. They dive into the mysteries of DNA, the part of each living cell that contains the codes for all inherited traits, from hair colour to webbed toes.

Geologists are down-to-earth scientists who study planets from surface to core. They dig our home planet – how it came to be, what happened to it as it got older and why it turned out the way it did. They probably keep pet rocks.

Neurologists, neurobiologists and other **neuroscientists** are nervy researchers, who like nothing better than experimenting with brains and nervous systems. That way they can figure out how they work and how to put them right when they go wrong.

Paleontologists spend a lot of their time digging up fossils that help them figure out who and what lived where and when long before anyone was around to keep records. They're also quite keen about rocks.

Parapsychologists are **psychic researchers** who study weird mental phenomena that defy normal physical explanation. They hope to find some explanations we can understand and trust for such oddities as telepathy, ESP or out-of-body experiences. Mainstream scientists are usually very dubious of the study of parapsychology.

Pathologists are doctors who usually only see patients after they've died. That's because dead bodies are full of clues to how diseases start and how they affect people.

Physicists are really good at maths, and like nothing better than filling blackboards and computer screens with equations that tell them how matter and energy get along together and other physical stuff like that.

Psychiatrists might ask you to stretch out on a couch so you can talk comfortably to them. They are medical doctors who specialize in mental illness, both treating people with it and doing research into its causes and cures.

Psychologists feel happiest when they're investigating the mind and how it works. They try to answer the question, *why do we act, think and feel the way we do?* Some psychologists treat people to help them understand their thoughts and feelings.
Behavioural psychologists and **animal behaviourists** study the things that humans and animals do, hoping it will help them understand what makes us all tick.

Statisticians love numbers. Ask them to do a survey of your neighbourhood and they'll not only tell you how many people live in it, but also how many people with brown eyes or lop-sided earlobes are likely to move into your neighbourhood in the next year.

Zoologists have a thing about animals. They try to figure out how many types of animals there are, who's related to whom, why they all look so different and how they all live. Zoology is divided into as many disciplines as there are creatures; for example, **ichthyologists** study fish

Index

Acknowledgements

The work of the following scientists provided the basis for the scary science in this book. If there's anything wrong with the way it's reported or used, the fault lies entirely with the author.

Animal Behaviourists
Peter Borchelt, B.F. Skinner, Sherwood Washburn

Anthropologists
Paul Bohannan, Grover Krantz

Astronomers
Frank Drake, Annie Jump Cannon, Clark Chapman, Christopher Chyba, Luke Dones, David Morrison, Ray Reynolds, Victor Clube, Bill Napier, Neil Comins, Dale Frail, James Kasting, Alexander Wolszczan, K. Michael Merrill, C. Robert O'Dell, Carl Sagan, James Scotti, Karen Strom, Stephen Strom, Scott Tremaine, George Wetherill, Daniel Whitmire, Michel Mayor, Didier Queloz, Geoffrey Marcy, Paul Butler.

Atmospheric Scientists
Walter Lyons, Eugene Westcott, Davis Sentman

Biologists
Frank Brown, Wilson Costa, Brian Hall, Julia Levy, Konrad Lorenz, John Napier, Rupert Sheldrake

Chemists
David Dolphin, Günter Gassman, Dieter Glindemann, Coenraad Hemker, Charles Kristensen, Helmut Tributsch

Computer Scientist
Larry Hodges

Dentists
Nathan Friedman, William Proffit

Engineers
Robert Jahn, Gert Pfurtscheller

Geneticist
Pragna Patel

Geologists
Walter Alvarez, Richard Grieve, Alan
Hildebrand, Wendy Wolbach

Historian
Mary Matossian

Ichthyologist
Marjorie Courtney-Latimer

Medical Doctors
Karen Farbman, Jerome Klein

Neuroscientists
Simon Baron-Cohen, Richard Cytowic,
Antonio Damasio, Michael Gazzaniga,
John Harrison, Hunter Jackson, Michael
Persinger, Jonathan Wolpaw

Nutritionist
John Milner

Paleontologists
Larry Marshall, Christopher McGowan

Pathologists
Nicholas Bellantoni, Paul Sledzik

Physicists
Peter Meijer, Grant McMillan, John
Schnurer, David Tumey, Joël Sternheimer

Psychologists
Daryl Bem, Susan Blackmore, Randolph
Blake, Linda Caporael, Richard Coss,
Mats Frederickston, Jack Gottlieb,
Charles Honorton, Arne Öhman, Leslie
Solyom, Nicholas Spanos

Psychiatrists
Carl Gustav Jung, John Mack, Barbara
Rothbaum, Philip Weinstein

Statistician
Christopher Scott

Zoologists
Jerry Harasewych, Desmond Morris

Photo Credits